AFTER BABEL

After Babel
CHRISTINE WEBB

PETERLOO POETS

First published in 2004
by Peterloo Poets
The Old Chapel, Sand Lane, Calstock, Cornwall PL18 9QX, U.K.

© 2004 by Christine Webb

The moral rights of the author are asserted in accordance with the Copyright, Designs and Patent Act, 1988

All rights reserved. No part of this publication may be reproduced, stored in a retrieval system, or transmitted, in any form or by any means, electronic, mechanical, photocopying, recording or otherwise without the prior permission in writing of the publisher.

A catalogue record for this book is available from the British Library

ISBN   1-904324-03-7

Printed in Great Britain by
Antony Rowe Ltd, Chippenham, Wilts.

ACKNOWLEDGEMENTS

Acknowledgements are due to the editors of *Smiths Knoll*, in which 'Journeyman' first appeared.

The author would also like to thank tutors on courses of the Arvon Foundation, and especially Carol Ann Duffy and Jackie Kay, for their help, advice and encouragement.

For Jackie Clarke

Contents

Page	
9	It was not the fruit
11	1912: The Visit to the Farm
12	Longshaw
14	Journeyman
15	Allotment
16	Chopping Wood
17	Gospel Truths
	1. GIANTS IN THOSE DAYS
	2. VISITATIONS
	3. MARTHA
	4. ACCOUNTING FOR THE PRODIGAL
	5. SEEING THINGS
23	The Midwife's Tale
24	Terms of Dissection
25	Absent: no good reason
27	Dramatis Personae: Seminar 1
28	Hall of Mirrors
30	Letters from my mother: Postcard
31	Letters from my mother: Shoe
32	Letters from my mother: Cheque
33	Letters from my mother: Trixie
35	Ivan
36	The Book
38	Her breathing
39	Freckle
40	Dark Matter
41	Going Ashore, Finnesnes
42	Metamorphosis
43	Models of Behaviour
44	A Question of Balance
45	'Fruit is light made flesh'
46	The Touch Pool
47	Deodar Cedar
48	Inch of Gold

49	Yew Hedge
50	Beyond Ringinglow
51	August, 1950
52	Voyage North: Sea Haikus
53	Countrywoman
54	Slipping Away
55	Viewing the Body
56	Away
57	At Wittenham Clumps
58	*From* The Elephant Boy
	1. THE CALIPH'S GIFT
	2. AS FOR THE ELEPHANT
	3. ARRIVAL
60	Aunt Em
61	Aunt May
62	Aunt Kit
63	Aubade: Auntie Lena at the washbasin
64	Ringing for Gopher
66	Newark Castle
67	Thread
69	Woman with a Pitcher of Milk
70	Recipe For a Folk Tale
72	The Box
74	After Babel
76	Nominal Aphasia

It was not the fruit

It was not the fruit she took
but the wood
not its flesh she chewed
but a pulpy fibre

(warm in that cavity
so various, ingenious
close to the brain
mother of language
thought shaper)

– spat out, finally
moulded and flattened
into rough leaves
a little bigger than the figs'
and drier

and for ink?
there were the experimental
berries, saps – ground
insects, even –
or the last resort,
the slow ooze
of red.

No problem of what
to say: creation
all around, bursting
into words... *In The
Beginning* ...
         A shadow
fell across the page as

she squatted, rapt – Women
don't write, he said

And screwed up her bible.

1912: The Visit to the Farm

And there the wrinkled cream stood on the milk
as thick as yellow ice, and you could cut it
with a knife, and the stone slabs were damp
and cool, like the cheeks of the cold field
mushrooms, the light dim as a cave

it was quiet too, even the low
contraltos of the cows or the rattle
of wheels was far off
                      and I knew
when I left the dairy there would be
hayfields outside, and a brown silk
stream to cool my ankles all summer
and no smoke, no trams
                    the city
was a life away
                    but forever
here the wrinkled cream stood on the milk
as thick as yellow ice, and you could cut it
with a knife

Longshaw

When are you going to marry me? The moor
stretched around them, its browns and purples
buzzing in the haze of August; a fawn bee
tilted a spike of heather... She looked from her shoe
up at his earnest face. The small moustache
was ridiculous (a sign of vanity in a man
she'd always said). Pause. He reached for her hand.
*Do you think you've known me long enough
to ask?*

This is their story. I've heard it both ways –
from her, who gave that question in answer (he
never mentioned that) and years later, after
her death, from him. *It was the first time we'd been
alone together,* she said. His version added:
*It was the first time I could get her
on her own, away from that blessed family.* (She
never mentioned that.)

She told everyone (I imagine) – the blessed
family, friends; showed the ring
he'd spent two months' wages on. He told
nobody till one Friday morning
in the workshop: *When are you going to get
married, Jack?* The perfect line: *Half-past ten
tomorrow, if you want to know.* Laughter:
You bloody liar.

So she married the workshop, the years
of rationing, his caution and anxiety,

the flat Midland town, her own exile;
and he married her laughter, the lilt
of her voice, the spring in her step, and
a mystery in her that eluded him –
never really knowing her well enough
to ask.

Journeyman

Packing up chisels, planes, neat as a surgeon,
he leaves his lit bench in the roaring workshop
(where the bandsaw once caught up Lije Jackson
and stripped him of everything but his boots
dropping him to bleed to death in the shavings)

and sets out, savouring the quiet night,
under the swaying shadows of streetlamps
pedal by pedal, over the boundary bridge
the wind clearing the sawdust from his nostrils
his brain still absorbed in the geometry

of staircases, until he reaches the street,
the fence, the kerb (swinging his leg over
the crossbar), the back door's blurred panel
(tapping the woodcurls out of his turn-ups)
the bacon-scented kitchen, my mother's kiss.

Allotment

The raspberries are sharp, cool, fitting my fingers
like thimbles. You teach me how to test and tweak them,
leave dangling the whitish inverted cones,
never damage the plants. Your hands are huge,
brown, with flat nails cut square. Earlier,
they have rustled through papery rows of peas,
bagged potatoes; all day before that
held steady the plane, the saw, fed blond
lengths into the shriek of the moulding
spindle. They are calm. I've watched them
flat-knotting bandages over torn knees,
pulling out splinters. I have not yet seen them
tremble. The thick arthritis of winter
is years away, still.

You clean your tools, load the bicycles.
Around us, the allotments smoke towards evening.
A train passes, trailing its vapour like time

– and takes half a century with it.
The raspberries ripen, tasting as fresh as ever.

Chopping Wood

Propped upstairs, he's using all his energy
to cough the pneumonia out of his lung.
The house is cold. It is Good Friday.
The livingroom fire will soon need lighting.

The kitchen breathes damp. Maybe the yeast is stale.
This batch of hot-cross buns won't rise.
Squeezing the dough into a sour ball,
slamming it down, you flare out of the house.

Wind knifes through the yard. The coalhouse door
flaps, yawns. In the gritty dark the axe
offers itself to oak, ash (a fast burner)
and blocks of deal with their smooth cheeks.

Hefting its weight, you swing into the heart
of the softwood, the clear notes whanging.
The faggots sculpt themselves, spring apart.
Your hands tingle. Soon the flames will be rising.

Gospel Truths

1. GIANTS IN THOSE DAYS

They shadowed every day, their stories closer,
realer than the news. Holy sandals scuffed
pavements, crunched the cindertrack to Golgotha.
The seaside's flatness was a Galilee ready
to erupt in storm, transfiguring the Lincolnshire
afternoon, their footprints inch by inch
disappearing in the slick anonymous sand.

I could reach out to touch them all – Peter
with his hot eyes and promises, John
leaning on God's shoulder, Mark running
through the olive-scented night in panic,
leaving his garment behind. In the dark a star
hung blinking over our shed, or a cock crew
from a neighbour's henhouse down the street.

It was not for a long time that I felt the absence
of women. There were some in the margins – anonymous,
asking for crumbs, bleeding, breaking their phial
of ointment, lying sick, raised from the dead
or waiting, dumbly, for stoning. A few had a name
but several Marys, it seemed, had been confused.
I was told this did not matter. They had their part.

Over the years the heroic footprints filled
with sea, lost their shape, faded at last
washed out by newer tides. The shining fish
slipped through the miracle net, or heaped
on the shore, grew dull, stank. Only the women's
voices rose now and then from the page
asking what it had all been for.

2. VISITATIONS

I'm too old for this, I thought as another lurch
of sickness scalded my throat. By then, we were used to
the empty space, the quiet: it's God's will
some women are barren. I had my compensations.
Aunt to the whole neighbourhood, I nursed
the sick, sewed for children, laid out our dead.
Zack had his priest work. We were content.

Love? It was quiet, a sleeper under a habit
of gestures and smiles. No demands. Just once
in a while, Zack would hoist himself up, I'd
spread myself, usually thinking of something
else. When my shows stopped coming, I simply
assumed, *that's it, then.* Was it relief?
Then I threw up, three mornings in a row.

Zack came back from the city. Couldn't speak.
What had happened that day while he stood
by the altar? He grunted, waved his arms, wept,
put his hand on my belly. I was afraid.
In the night I dreamt of fire, of blood,
a figure shouting in a desert, then the head
sliced from the body. I was sick again.

Six months gone. The baby was kicking
as my cousin arrived. I knew by her face
before she said a word. *God has blessed you*
I said. Words poured out of us both, a Jordan
of images washing us away, our smallness
swept along in some huge Otherness. Why?
When she left, I was exhausted.

Birth. *Call him John,* I said, the name
surfacing on a wave of pain. Zack pointed,

wrote on a slate: *John, John, John*
– then stammered his story. I listened: did
the angel he saw visit me too?
                         The boy
is strange already, gazing towards a horizon
of emptiness, giving himself elsewhere.

3. MARTHA

I was elbow-deep in grease. That lamb
(in a herb crust) doesn't exactly cook
itself. And there's a pan to scour after.
Then the home-made bread, bitterleaf salad
(lightly dressed with oil) not to mention
figs, plums, apricots, almonds and a couple
of bottles of wine. I didn't notice him
(or anyone) refusing second helpings
nor minding me dodging about with dishes,
spooning gravy, cutting extra bread.
After dinner, there's our Mary sitting
literally at his feet – he has the one
comfortable chair, she's hunched on a cushion
drinking it all in. I'm doing a quick sweep
round the kitchen, hoping to get back to the chat
half listening to them while I go on stacking
pots. Then here he is in the doorway:
'Mary's made the best choice,' he says.
I stare. Is this a joke? My good lamb
hardly out of his mouth, beard stained with gravy:
'You should prioritise more. Don't spend so long
in the kitchen.' And he's on his way,
picking a thread of meat from his teeth. God.

4. ACCOUNTING FOR THE PRODIGAL

When Sim left, I took over the accounts.
It'd always been his job: Jos was hopeless with figures –
the crops, the beasts, were what he loved, using
his muscles. Father'd never got the hang of a calculator,
let alone a spreadsheet. Things were tight at first.
With Sim's share gone (and no word from him – might
have been dead, for all we knew) we had to re-mortgage:
had some very thin times, with the bank on our backs
and the neighbouring farms watching, just in case
there was a killing.

But we turned the corner.
I began to enjoy the business: gradually
we expanded, bought in stock, paid off
some of the loans: I even treated myself
to a new software package.

                      So there we are, last back end:
a record harvest, the bank cautiously pleased
and a deal in view: a dozen young beasts earmarked
for the autumn sale. I'm running the end-of-year
returns, just thinking *If we go on like this
we'll pay off that mortgage early*. Then (from some
cyber-café two continents away) an e-mail:
Dad – I fucked up. Coming home. Sim.

Father's like a man possessed. Butchers the best
calf from the sale herd, orders in booze by the gallon,
galumphs round the place humming. Jos looks
like murder. They have a row. Somehow Father
talks him round. I stay out of it, trying to work out
whether Sim will be let back in, what this will do
to the business. Eventually Father shambles in,
looks over my shoulder as the machine purrs –

then says what he's not said now for two years:
I sh'think Sim'll be able to pick up from here.
You've done pretty well for a woman.

                                      I smile,
log off. A few days later, I take my skills
elsewhere, leave them to muddle along. That's why
you don't find me in the story.

5. SEEING THINGS

All the water in my body had run out
by the time he died. At first
I couldn't look at all, just kept my eyes
fixed on the little ridges my feet
had scuffed in the stained dust. But the shadow
fell on my bent neck like the sun, so
hot I had to look up. Then I was consumed
in looking: the muscles at full stretch, bones
edged as if they'd score the skin, the face
unrecognizable, eyes and mouth holes punched
into emptiness. And the hands (my hands
remembered their touch) splintered, pulped.
Couldn't look again. Had to. It got dark
but still hot. Dry thunder. The earth shook.
The end was a long time coming.

Interlude of good smells. Cave-smell, earthy
and cold. Winding the steeped bandages, sharp,
resinous. Walking away, the grass aromatic
with sap and dew. No tears: the stone
– its smell heavy, dense, neutral – had sealed
me up too.

Now the city is full of rumours, visions
multiplying like an infection. The men
are feverish, gathering, shouting in hoarse
excitement. I keep away. I too
had my moment of ecstasy, meeting
a dream in the long grass at dawn –
that tricky light when trees look like men
walking. He came towards me from the edge
of the sunrise.

    But it was only the gardener.

The Midwife's Tale

I saved the afterbirths for Mr FitzHughes –
Don't forget, Sister, whenever you've time –
plum-purple, plum-plush-soft... though what with blood,
water, cries (some women shriek like pigs –
It's good pain, I tell them) and then the soft
head appearing, screwed up face, the tiny
soles of the feet... and that first high wail
strung out on a breath like the bloody cord –
there's enough to do without packing up placentas
for Mr Mighty FitzHughes. But I usually did.
It's his research, I thought, important, maybe.

Twenty years he was there. *You must come to tea,
Sister, when I've retired.* Not many say that:
flattered, I admit. And the house – full of small
expensive things. *Now, Sister, the greenhouse*
(while his wife made tea) – *I especially
want to show you the grapes.* Black, full –
cut me a fistful. *Try these, Sister... and look
down: see that rich soil? Fertile, aren't they,
those afterbirths you saved? Foot of every vine –
nothing beats them.*
       The grapes were almost
bursting in my hand – purple-red, swollen.
I thought, Mrs Jones's placenta... Never
fancied grapes since.

Terms of Dissection

Anatomy is another kind of poetry
with structures rhyming, thigh by thigh,
shoulder by shoulder, the ribs a shortened
sonnet, perfectly interlaced. Lungs
perform their powerful stanzas, kidneys
recite couplets. Every body delivers
the same lines, all subtly different:
femur, scapulae, vertebrae.

I'd imagined the head, with its ruined
personhood, might horrify
but found the same calm analysis
unpacked volumes of metaphor –
columns of images ascending, descending,
kernels of meaning still embedded
(cerebellum, hippocampus)
in that pale magnificent walnut.

Late in the course (my knife was confident now,
a detached appraiser) I came to the hand
(carpals, metacarpals). I picked it up. The knuckles
were swollen. It had washed, scratched an itch,
stroked a lover, a child, lifted a fork,
turned pages – who knows? played the violin.
It lay in mine, waiting.
                        I stood for a moment
as if reading its lifeline.

Absent: no good reason

Miss, I saw Marie yesterday.

Marie was a right laugh. Didn't stay long
(didn't stay anywhere long) what with
fighting, nicking stuff, mouthing the teachers
and not just mouthing – went for Smithy once
straight at the throat. Gave us all a treat.
She was my best mate for a time. A good laugh.

But not yesterday. Weren't much laughing yesterday.

She got pregnant last summer. Never let on
not to anyone for a long time, not till
she'd got a belly on her like a pig's
backside. By then she was round her nan's –
said she reckoned her dad would go ballistic.
We kept in touch – she'd like phone most weeks.

Didn't see her though, not till yesterday.

At first I was pissed off when her nan rang.
She'd been in labour two days – why hadn't no one
told me? Then she goes, 'Marie's in a bad way'
and all day I was thinking about blood, pain.
Couldn't settle. At teatime she rang again.
She'd had the baby. It'd lived five minutes.

Me and some mates went to the funeral yesterday.

Fucking cold day. We thought we ought to wear
something black. Stood shivering. Sky was grey.
People in the streets getting on with stuff

like nothing mattered. There was this little sad box, and a great load of flowers.
Marie didn't speak once. We came away.

Miss, I haven't got a note for yesterday.

Dramatis Personae: Seminar 1

This oblong of print, neatly columnar
does not square with the rough circle
of faces perching here, alert
with expectation or anxiety.
Aaronovitch, George, has not arrived
– he will burst in, furious-haired
three weeks later, having missed
the first act (Explication).
Cahoun, Chris, scarlet with acne
will have left by then for Management
and Business Studies (Resolution).
The list is corrupt, a Bad Quarto –
mis-spelling Lascelles, omitting Ormeroyd –
and will need annotations later:
Tilling, Charlotte, who will sob
behind her long hair in Week Five
(Catastrophe) doesn't know
this autumn is chosen by her parents
for their separation. Jobson,
Greg, will miss class after class,
heedless of warning. And Beckett,
Samantha, is permanently off-stage
waiting for a cue. We may as well
begin without her.

Hall of Mirrors

And now, says the guide, you will travel
into the past. Lights off! Click:
thick cloth on eyeballs, and the hall
of mirrors is an underground chamber
where we are entombed upright –
so many terracotta soldiers
who will be discovered forty years from now.
The walls are slipping, no longer solid
as time dissolves them, and Versailles belongs
to Petain, Clemenceau, Napoleon,
spins back through Bourbons, Capets, Gauls
until ice-ages re-solidify
in terraces, or swamps quiver
beside an older river-course.
You could lick the mirrors now, and taste mist.

Out of the mist a curved searching hand
cups itself round a bottom, tight
as a barnacle. 'It's rude down there, Pat'
said Auntie, once, as the child fished in her knickers
for a handkerchief, briefly skimming
that smooth mound where nothing
could ever grow. Pat shifts in the dark, now,
wriggling away from rudeness:
the hand's not big, could be as familiar
as sisters' laps to bottoms in the winter bed –
but the toughness Pat feels is not sisterly,
the clutch a bit sticky, but not a child
gripping an ice-cream. The fingers spread.
Time does not travel, but stiffens
to a halt, filling the crowded darkness.

Then lights punch back, and mirrors swim

up from the depths. The hand's floated away.

Out in the dizzying light French voices crash
on the shore of the afternoon. A band is hurling
notes that spray on the gravel. 'Rude',
they say, 'rude'. Aunt buys ice-creams.
'Well. That was something. What mirrors.
Now lick that drip, and mind you don't get sticky.'
Pat licks, licks. Sticky. The mist, the mirrors.
And then is sick, beside the immaculate lawns.

Letters from my mother: Postcard

Grey and white, the Princess, the Duke and their neatly
combed children, squinting at the sun on a lawn
as big as a field. 'Seen Buckingham Palace, too,
from a bus,' she wrote on the back, 'though they didn't
ask me in for tea.'

                                               We scrutinised
every detail – the exotic postmark, *MIDDX*,
our formal names, The Misses Webb – ate it
with breakfast, handing it back and forth, licking
our fingers, then propped it by the oblong clock
we'd both learnt to tell the time by. 'Back for tea
on Friday,' she wrote. We counted the meals between

– at which alone our father would preside, oddly
amputated without her. 'Tell Daddy I've written
to him,' she wrote. But when it came, he kept
her letter in his waistcoat pocket, smiling.
We knew their hands and faces as intimately
as our own, but sensed something unknowable –
closer than the Princess but as mysterious.
We let him read our postcard but just glimpsed
over his shoulder her first line, 'Dearest Jack'.

Letters from my mother: Shoe

'I don't know what we're going to do about
Katherine's shoe,' her letter began. 'That wretched
dog of Peter's bit the toe right through
last Thursday. She's had to go to school in her sandals.
Of course he was there on the doorstep the same evening
offering to pay for a new pair, but I couldn't let him –
though where we're going to find fifty-nine
and eleven, I don't know. Now don't you go
trying to send me money – we shall manage.

'Your father's late at the allotment again, though it's
nearly dark – I think he must be worshipping
those cabbages. I made a nice rhubarb
pie today, had a letter from Dorothy.
Such trivia!

      'Later, excuse scrawl, Tuesday –
Katherine took the shoe to that cobbler's in
Bargate, and he stitched the toe for sixpence.
Would you believe it? Such a weight off my mind.
A beautiful crisp morning here. I bet it's
lovely in Cambridge. Enjoy your university
years, dearest child. They go so quickly.'

Letters from my mother: Cheque

Your father's waited five years to see what
profit he'd get from that field – how like his family
to end up with the only few acres in the village
that nobody could make money from: Lacey Green
indeed! – lacy's about the size of it, more marsh than
solid from what I gather. Still it's a mercy
he never went into farming for how he'd have coped
with the uncertainty I dread to think – as it is
we have a drama every year about the potatoes.

The cheque anyway has now arrived from the great sale –
a pretty miserable sum too after all these years.
Mind you, if that petrol company had ever built
a filling station on it that would have been
a different story, but oh no, it's just the Government's
compulsory purchase for us, and that blessed bypass.
Well it came on Friday, and very pleased we were
to get it. Sunday evening he was just going to give it me
to take in to the Bank, and could we find it? Of course
he was sure I'd lost it – I swore it was in the drawer
with the overheads, but in the end nothing would do
but to traipse outside down the yard. There we were
in our Sunday best rooting in the bin, and lo and behold
there was the envelope torn up neatly – and blow me,
the wretched cheque, also in pieces. We found
all of them except the bit with the bloke's
signature, so we've had to write to him and explain
what has happened. Now, as they say, we await
developments. Your father was livid.

Letters from my mother: Trixie

I saw Trixie in the market. She sent her love.
She was always fond of you – I remember her
visiting with strawberries that July morning
just after you were born, in the middle of the war.
She swept you up, kissed the little strawberry
mark on your bottom. Don't forget her birthday.

*

Trixie called. One of her eyes is sore
– looks small and red, too – she'd not have mentioned it
if I'd not asked her. I was just slicing some melon:
how I remember the first one after the war
we cut up in her kitchen, laughing, squealing
at the scent, the juice... She sent her love.

*

Trixie rang me: she's having that eye out
– no sight in it, very disfiguring – oh, if eyes
ever danced, hers did. And laughter! Can you
remember – you were four – pushing the glass
baubles in that blue bowl? I can see your face
now, and hers watching you. She sent her love.

*

Went to see Trixie – not been right since that wretched
eye business, and now she's so thin, like a hot
fragile bird when I hugged her. 'I'll be glad when this
is over,' she said. Kept stroking the fur on the winter
gloves Bill's bought her, and smiling, but I
can't see her lasting till winter. She sent her love.

*

Bill rang Sunday – would I come and see Trixie
while she was lucid. I said, 'What about
next week?' 'Eh, love', he said 'next week
she'll not be here.' I got straight on the bus, without
even a hat. Sat with her an hour, just holding
her hand. I think she knew me. I gave her your love.

Ivan

North Street: striped shadows –
a day in the city of
flecked sunlight, flying clouds.

At the foot of crumbling
steps, in a shabby room
filling it somehow with light:
a figure of folk-tale, cross-
legged in the immemorial
manner of tailors, the dangling
tape round the neck, swift
fingers speeding a thread.

The dark heart of an unseen
radio pulsed with quiet
words, music, pauses –
laying down warp and weft
across the room, patterning
the air: meanwhile his needle
darted through woven fabric,
a damsel-fly improbably
bathing in the light
at the heart of the city.

Decades are past, and he
dust with them, but still
in his cave the golden man
is plying his magic needle.

The Book

Wolfing down the last page, sitting
in a low chair as you passed by
I looked up from the book you'd
lent me: *Well, what do you
think?* you asked; and as I
replied *Marvellous,* that huge
smile lit your face. A surge
of heat rocked my stomach, as if
receiving some intoxication
it couldn't neutralize or digest:
O no, not again,
I thought as the wave hit
my brain. But it was,
of course, too late.
      I left
the book lying and instead
began to study first the book
of your face – its leaves of
sorrow, passages of hope,
flashes of joy – and then of
your mind, which at first was
coded, a Rosetta stone
whose key took me months to find.
Found, though, it unlocked
that other book too which
by now I desired so much –
golden volume of your body.
I returned to it again
and again, to read, devour,
absorb, learn by heart.

      I've been
Studying that text,

living on that substance
ever since, but it's assimilated
now, built into my tissues.
Holy book. Daily bread.

Her breathing

I've got used to your asthma, over time:
the slow step, the long or quickdrawn breath,
sudden notes high like a bird's or
a mad concertina, an eccentric flute
in the next room or a chamber of my ear.

There've been the nights fighting for breath, when at
each gasp I've congratulated you, *good,
good,* as if a prize for achievement – and
at the same time I've found myself holding
breath too, my lungs tight with your effort.
At dawn we've looked at each other, not in
triumph but sweatily, survivors.

Mostly you live with this energy of speed,
timing your pace to its grip, eluding, grappling,
and I grow used to the long sigh, the engine
steaming up, herald of your approach
across a space – shop, concert-hall, bed.
Your breath haunts me like the sea. I think
of words to breathe: inspire; *suspire; atmen.*
Sometimes alone in the garden or in a distant
city I hear a breath approaching – turn
surprised when no one's near. Perhaps you're thinking
of me, as I of you. Just go on. *Atmen.*
Amen.

ERRATUM

1st line of final stanza (line 13) should read:

Mostly you live with this enemy of speed,

Freckle

The freckle on your toe's become a mole.
That summer kiss the sun's tongue flicked
out to touch you toast-brown with, still
wombfast – that dot you hoarded, your own
warm gold – suddenly's a winter scab:
lumpish, crusted, like the crumbling curds
of a tiny cauliflower, frost-bitten. We look
at it in the flat grey light of January, and
you carry it warily to the doctor.

February, you're limping, your toe a neat
cone, candystriped flesh and white.
Keep Your Wound Dry: awkward uni-
ped, you can't vault into the bath, but wash
slowly, in portions. Hobbling into clinics,
pissing and purging, you learn your kidney
and colon are fine. We grin, tell each other
They can cure melanoma nowadays.

Small daffodils come out under the kitchen
window, early. It snows. We look for omens.

Dark Matter

Some days, I can't summon up a smile.
Blaming you for the journey you've been forced
to make, I automate my answers, nod,
sweep through rooms on a mission, ticking lists.
Tenderness, caresses, our long interrogative
gaze – vanished down some mineshaft
of the past. What evidence emerges
is peripheral – sheets hung, bread cut,
soup ladled, and the house not so much
run as levered from waking to sleeping.
This is dark matter, only to be inferred
by its effects on what surrounds it: if
it's love, there'll be a day to be thankful.

Going Ashore, Finnesnes

Going ashore, I would bring you
a rose, but roses don't
grow in this town: all buds are
clenched tight; grass can't

get beyond khaki. I'd find you
a pebble, but cement blocks
line the harbour; grit sprays up
from dry-frozen wheel-tracks.

So I bring you the sway of a frond
caught by the sea-wall there;
I bring you the gloss of the sea;
I bring you a lungful of air.

Metamorphosis

In memory of Ted Hughes

Heard you were dead; took down your *Tales from Ovid*.

Hercules roared off the page, wrestling
Trees, rocks as he died; the Bacchantes
Wrenched Pentheus' sinews apart, dis-
Membering him like a chicken; softly, Midas
Drooled idiot gold, spat barren
Apple-pips.
         These destructions
Shadowed others, more intimate, and howled
In other forms, fangs, claws, the oily birth-
Puddle of those born dead.
                      Old shape shifter,
You lurk, pike, otter, in the dark
Richness of my mind; the sky of four
Decades quivers with your winds and wings:
Hawk hangs overhead, or crows
Torn like black paper in the gale toss
Your words away...
                I must go out,
Savour the late sun, the scattered kindle
Of leaves, breathe in a new element
That now holds you as you held it, broad-
Casts you over and over the land
Seeding us with your cells' wealth.

Models of Behaviour

Inside each ant a microcosmic chip
directs six feet to walk like millions.
They weave inscrutably along soily furrows
staggering with eggs, those fat pillowcases.
Like lumberjacks they tackle a dead wasp
hewing off its leg-branches, sawing the trunk
through. Economic with language, they obey
only those imprinted circuits they were hatched with.

The wrens, meanwhile, have gone insane
with competition. Male hyper-sopranos
broadcast from the laurel, the apple-tree, the oak.
A female adjudicates; inspects nests critically
before committing herself. Big with the future
she models patience in a warm cup of twigs
while her mate, entrepreneur, invests in bigamy.

Out in the field the dance of genes has patterned
the red and white coats of the cows, and scattered
them sisterly across the slope. One leans
her warm flank against another's, perhaps tenderly.
They do not look for mirrors in the universe.

A snail persists up the wall. The cat lounges.
Clover opens itself drunkenly to the sun.
An ant stabs my foot.

A Question of Balance

Centred in a ring of lights, attached
by electrodes to a Swiss robot,
the lamprey's brain turns to the light

(its first function overwritten –
to keep its owner upright
in the vast salt tideflow)

If one of the robot's eyes is masked
the brain becomes confused
but quickly learns to adjust

while on the other side of the world
a human brain, disrupted by some neural
accident, waits to discover

whether this patch, snipped
from one edge of the universe
can mend a hole elsewhere

It is a miracle
but the lamprey in its cool salt fluid
rich with oxygen, turning

obediently from light to light, wonders
where all the dark has gone
where all the dark has gone

'*Fruit is light made flesh*'

Andrew Marvell knew it, seeing the oranges
as golden lamps in the Bermudan groves
of green night. Look here, too, where a lesser
summer's brilliance has infused the plums
with this miraculous ichor, offering
mouthfuls of honey to the palates of wasps,
birds and the rasping tongues of snails.
Last month's opals, hard and scentless,
have turned to rose, amber, a purple bloom
hovering over the surface, wild yeasts
so fragile they fracture as the thumb rubs them.
The gleam in the leaves! The glow between the branches!
Stand transfixed on the ladder, drink in the scent,
feel your tongue bud with desire, before you
reach to break the web of light that holds them.

*The Touch Pool**

Pancakes, freckled,
maculate, dark
moles on creamy

flesh, or stippled
straw-pale pinheads
interlaced with brown:

these are the rays.
Chameleon, they slip
seamlessly under

gravel, unseen,
then skim, undulate
upwards, to lip

our alien fingers
at the pool's edge
and idle away.

At night – the pool
an island in the hall's
depths – do they rise

to nuzzle at our echoes
and sip the quiet
– or do they move

in a dance with darkness
whirled by the rhythms
of unguessed-at tides?

[Part of an aquarium where visitors are allowed to touch the fish]

Deodar Cedar

The crows have deserted the cedar. Last year, a nest
still rocked, cupped, in a crook of the dry branches
but no one brooded in it, nor added twigs
in raucous defiance of the chimneytop daws
nor did those challenge for that more desirable
swaying residence. They recognised deadness
in the stiff gestures, the total absence
of the least hint of green.
                                  Summers, the drift
of needles once populated the air
with a glinting shower; small cones ripened
above the rough grass, where a cloud of shadow
and scent hovered. The monochrome of winter
was teased by that dark fur, on the dourest afternoon
still hoarding colour. Now, it is only shape,
but still eloquent of another world: the field
framed through its bare arms takes on a new
angle; its script translates the sky.
                                      Exotic
stray into this landscape of hawthorn and oak
it could not flourish long, but in its decline
sustains funguses, insects, the resonant mining
of woodpeckers. We watch it, shrewdly calculate
its angles of likely descent, wonder whether
to drop it before it drops us; leave it to the winter
mists, the mistle-thrushes' rusty calls,
the slow decisions of rain.

Inch of Gold

I was sorry your bees died. Every summer
your envoys have negotiated the slope
between us: the rise of the field's not been
too much for them, the distance within their span.
Somehow my riches of lavender, rosehedge, weeds
have nourished your broods, and stretched
across a half-mile this furry humming line.

We tell bees our deaths, but can't warn them
of the small messenger that carries theirs.
The hives are cold now; the last inch of honey
crystallizes. I can't bear to eat
the gold at the bottom of the jar.

Yew Hedge

Antitheses: a thicket of dry fingers
Interlocked, like green fishbones, and dusty
With ancient drought; hidden inside it, chirrs,
Flutters, beakfuls of movement, solid glitter
Of a watching eye. The hedge pulses, alive,
Unobserved; empties at human approach
With a tiny clatter.

                   In it there have been:
Two goldcrests, kindling spurts of spark-
Colour flicking twig to twig; a ragged
Thrush, feather's-breadth escapee
From cat's claws; the cat itself, pouring
Through tangles its neat elongation of fur;
The architectural theory of spiders
Realised in finespun; dead wasps, parcelled.
Underneath, in the cool sift of grains,
Lie tiles, shards, broken guttering, half bricks.

You'd think hedge and soil alike were barren.
But no: yew-berries, scarlet blobs of wax,
Seal autumn, and great limbs of murderous
Bramble writhe through the dimness, luscious with fruit.

Beyond Ringinglow

For Katherine

The moor is unemphatic, makes no claim
to be extraordinary. Its rough heather
stretches in clumps and tangles, intergrown
with bilberries, sharp indigo studs
that catch the sun's warmth on their round cheeks.
Shadows tear across the earth as the wind
scoops up and hurls its armfuls of air.

The bones of the earth are strong here, pressing up
against foot or hand. But bend down, interrogate
the cup of a single harebell. Watch
the thorn tree lean against the wind, recover,
rooted, rooted. From the far height a curlew
signals its two syllables, and maps
the acreage of moor, small streams winking,
pillars of balanced rocks caught in the gleam
where rain and sun have woven a net of light.

August, 1950

A dark cloud on the right, swerving and weaving
in figures of eight over the evening woods
forming, re-forming – sashes and ribbons
plaiting a monochrome dance, high in the air.

Grandfather, father, child, we stand in the road:
too far for the whirr, the beat of wings to reach us
out of the high oscillations inside the cloud –
and not a screech from the beaks, not a yawp, not a burble.

On their unseen dance-floor the starlings shimmy
partnered by thousands, wingtip to wingtip, a feather's
width away, but never clipping or brushing
even a filament ... And the cloud unravels.

We turn to each other, and find we are standing on tiptoe.

Voyage North: Sea Haikus

Rippling, dimpling, sheer
seersucker, silk sheet, subtly
tugged by the tide's hands.

Under its smooth skin
are swaying triangles, falls,
peaks birds can sit on.

Heavy roll: the breasts,
thighs of some immense she-sea-
god turning, surging.

Wolfwaves: grey-backed, white-
open-throated, rearing against
shipsides resisting.

Horizons buck, buckle,
tilt, up-heave obliquely, can't
stay horizontal.

Slide between sudden
islands: roar, bucketing sub-
side now to silence.

A bright cloud steers
its ponderous reflection
on the dark mirror.

Laced edges slip, thread
under, over: infinite
reticulations.

Midnight light's pearly
translucence rests unsleeping
on sheets of opal.

Countrywoman

walks every day in the lane, breathing
the sweet brown reek of cows, watching
goose-grass knit the hedges together
hearing the falsetto wheeze from
a wren's nestful, thumbing the heavy
heads of the grasses. Companioned by her ghosts –
father, mother, the rough flank of a dog –
she is not solitary, ignores the passing
cars whose drivers will not taste the lime
or elder pollen brushing the cheeks of the air.

Slipping Away

Slipping one morning so uncharacteristically
away, you left without explanation, nor –
stranger still – have sent word later, not even a
sardonic comment on what you found there (wherever
that is). Where is your laugh? the calling
horn of your voice?

And where, now, can we find you? I've looked
everywhere. The garden is empty except of
snowdrops (you planted them) and in the kitchen
stand bowls and cups you made, but aren't using
today, again. Your books lean together, or open
at poetry that I've not heard you quote
for days. And you haven't hidden mischievously
in the wardrobe, though it trails your glowing
rusts and oranges from swinging hangers.

At night I see you disjointedly in strange
houses or streets, only in the morning
returning to absence. You haven't spoken now
for over a week. I keep expecting to see
your prow of a nose forging through the winter
air, to put my arms round your frailness and
then be startled by the sharp relish of
your latest saying.
                        But you've found
a new way to surprise me.

Viewing the Body

The road admits nothing. Dealing out its small change –
catkins, the tender pink of willow
tips near the river (waterline high
again) – it can't persuade itself
of anything graver: your absence at its end
is irrelevant. I can't agree
but can't, yet, find the way to prove it
wrong.

                    And here we are. The house too
is ignorant, full of your echoes. Sunlight
falls on angles that retain your prints:
an inch of tapestry unworked, a brush-stroke
missing. On letters about you but no longer
to you. On empty shoes.

                        So at last
we go to find you, in the low-roofed shed
across the grey yard, beyond doors and doors
out of the sunlight, and the last door
opening silently suddenly shows
the not-you you've become, in a shiny
box you mustn't untidy. Your curved hands are cold
shells, the fragile relics of an ancient world.

You have closed your mouth on your secret.

Away

Like a bird you simply fell one day
out of the winter air: was it too thin,
dry? Or was your heart swollen,
labouring? – some incongruity
between them anyway.

I feel queer was all you said
before the last, fluttering drop:
no simple splash from cold tap,
nor bleeping, sophisticated
systems could pierce that dead

quiet of the passing hours
where you travelled further and
further through the strange land
relinquishing the body that was hers
and all we thought was ours

for an *its*. Its silence,
its stillness, its undramatic
sustained refusal to make
the least vestige of response.
Finally, its absence.

At Wittenham Clumps

The plan was to scatter you
on the ancient slopes
lose you along the hill
and up the airstreams.

We'd imagined sunlight
fat pillars of cloud
a sky full of scents
and you sifting yourself

over the grasses
and the bright eyes of dandelions.
We'd find the words to capture
and release your spirit.

A high wind barrelling
the clouds across the hill
took our breath away.
Tackling the slopes

with energetic cries
were robust strangers
into whose path
you would blow, to lodge

in folds of cloth and skin –
dust in the tender crevices
of lips and eyes,
gritty snot in noses.

We left the box sealed
as we turned away.
All the drive back
I heard you laughing.

From *The Elephant Boy*

(Three poems from a sequence based on the gifts of the caliph of Baghdad to the Emperor of the West. These gifts included an elephant.)

1. THE CALIPH'S GIFT

There was a water-clock, a miracle
of balances, glitter, the slow escape of time,
perfected in Baghdad or in Byzantium:
no-one in the west would comprehend it.
The third camel carried it indifferently –
pacing steadily, the great knees flexing and bending,
the pads planting themselves on stone, on sand,
trekking, tracking. Packed round with silks
their colours named for further gifts, saffron, turquoise –
the clock lay at the heart of the treasure, never
jolted, all the long swaying journey. Across mountain
passes, over the swelling backs of sea-
waves that bucked and tossed, the clock
slept. It would wake, in time.

2. AS FOR THE ELEPHANT

...it joined the company
later, its great ears drooping
limp flags on a windy day – patient,
tamed, accustomed from calfdom
to its twiglike keepers, the shrill scrape
of their voices, their insect jerkiness
and inventive cruelties. Tempted at times
to tread on them, to put an end to misery,
'Abul Azaz,' it told itself, 'you must
be generous in your giant life to these
grasshoppers you and the trees outlive.'
Alone among the travellers, it smelled

the true nature of the boy. Wary recognition
flowered between them, as they crossed skyline
after skyline.

3. ARRIVAL

Aachen. The court. The Franks, barbaric,
bristling with weapons, sprouting hair
like men grown from trees. The Emperor,
stiff from decades of campaigns, towering
over his nobles. Limped to the high seat,
called us before him. Golden beard
in the reddened face, eyes like blue sparks
missing nothing. Chewing one finger.

Isaac the Jew, sole survivor
of the three ambassadors (Berthold dead
of the flux in Baghdad, Mergar of snakebite) –
bowed low. Their language clotted
in his mouth, grated in the throat
but the word for elephant came out clear.
Then – the Emperor up, the court parting
like the sea before the Law-Giver –
banked waves of armour, glistening
leather – the Emperor striding, pulling
his stiff leg, shouting, all running after
and erupting into the courtyard.

The elephant stood quiet. It chewed a bundle
of grasses. The spring sunshine warmed
its hide. No hurry. Its head swung
round, the trunk a leisurely curve.
The eyes examined the golden man, who
stared at the grey hill of its flank.
Then he reached out a ringed hand
and the elephant blew into it. Softly.
They stood together, absorbed. Only
then did the Emperor notice the boy.

Aunt Em

There was Aunt Em. She was earth mother:
baked her own bread, made porridge
lemoncurd gravy biscuits
sewed worn sheets sides to middle
gave her youngest sister hints about
sex, sang contralto in the chapel. Shirts
and china rose brilliant from her soap-foamed
hands, more gnarled each year. She sat down
seriously in the library, choosing
her books with pursed lips, nodding
at her pencilled list, the fragile bun
of her hair quivering, skewered
with pins. Fifty years she ruled
kitchen and family with loving
labour and sharp-eyed reproof. I see her
eternally brandishing the blade
of the handle-less breadknife, making a point
in some argument, as she cut the bread
on returning from chapel, with her hat still on.

Aunt May

There was Aunt May. She was Hecate,
hell-cat, thin and wiry
with hair that jetted sparks. She scoured
pans with a furious wrist, alert
for specks that could offend her eye

The chisel of her gaze laid bare
the world's malice, engraving 'fickle',
'gone funny', 'can't trust her'
on the tombs of her friendships

She kicked her legs high in their thin
stockings, skittering at a ball
challenging us to compete
in the concrete yard where the drain
fumed from its weekly disinfectant

Even her gifts had teeth, and would bite you
later. She never forgot a price

In dreams still the black snakes
of her hair tie my hands down

Aunt Kit

Aunt Kit, divinity, freckled with gold,
blue gaze stately. She sailed majestic
with hoover and shopping. Bank clerks straightened
their ties on her entry. Her observations,
godlike, could scorch: *Folks don't have to like me,
just to remember.*

She mocked sisters, could lash lounging shop
assistants: *Do you work here, or are you
just decoration?* A dachshund – its heavy
tool wagging to the sleek waddle –
drew her mouth awry: *Can't the creature
put on some knickers?*

A child in her paradise house, I savoured
her thin bread and butter. Mornings, we scrubbed
her kitchen table, weeping with soap
and laughter, capping each other's rhymes,
helpless to explain our joy to her stout
Jupiter, my uncle.

In her sea-gowns of blue and turquoise
she rides the waves of memory,
immortal with her dangerous laughter.
Her hats were crowns. Even the grey
months of cancer couldn't extinguish
her golden spirit.

Aubade: Auntie Lena at the washbasin

Balances on one purpled foot, the other
scuffing off her slipper from the heel,
lurches to slop boiling gouts
into the cracked basin, dumps
the kettle too near the feet,
claws her rings off, strangles a flannel
– punishing face, arms, her breasts'
flaccid lemons, the scanty hairs
of *down below* – but cannot reach the domed
hump of her back. A pepper of talc
and 'Bob's your uncle'. In damp pyjamas
she grunts her way back through the kitchen, frowning
as she imagines next door's lovers
parting in the rosy flush of dawn.

Ringing for Gopher

(This legend of the man who lost his way and was saved by the sound of the church bells belongs to the town of Newark, where 'ringing for Gopher' is still done every year on the six Sundays before Advent)

Versions differ. He was, all agree,
out somewhere on the fens – maybe Farndon,
or further north towards Muskham, or westward
near the bend in the river by Kelham. Benighted
in autumn and fog, alert to catch the first
sibilant of that deadly speech of the marsh
that draws lives underwater. The mist
wiped his mind blank with its sponge.

Already old by Victoria's time, the story
surfaces into print from these marshy
origins, mouths passing it on, some clothing it
in eighteenth-century breeches and wig, some
in a vague mediaeval garment that disintegrates
across the centuries. Like Robin Hood, Gopher
has many guises; the fen, with the greenwood,
ubiquitously vanishing into legend.

A crabbed, creased paper in Bruges, heavy
and fragile, lists Jann Goffayr, Englishman,
as having his goods confiscated – one bale
of furs and one small cask – and sold, whether
to pay a fine, or debts, or customs dues
we don't know.
But now, perhaps, he exists,
trading between Flanders and the flat English
Midlands, speaking the dialect of Chaucer.

Out of the murk he tramps, with his mule
and its load, on some homeward journey. Fog thickens.
The sourwater reek rises. The skin of man and beast

prickle with fear. Then cutting across the dusk
Bim-bam-bim-bam-bom, bim-bam-bim-bem-bam-bim:
the bronze voices of the bells ring out, the mist
shifts. He senses his right road, strikes out
for the town, an inn, shelter, food, fire.

Centuries later, as the October chill descends,
we ring for Gopher still. Bim-bam-bom-bom.

Newark Castle

One dish of river eels, and King John
choked on slime, retching
in a last struggle for air
– but there's no room
(the guide admits) we can be sure
was his death chamber. He'd lost
his baggage and packhorses
in the Wash, but made it
here, only to fade out, eyes dimming
as mists swallowed the landscape, and the river
washed down his vomit and ran on.

Under the crumble of these walls
the green ribbon slides still
carrying away each moment
with the muddy fish, weeds and plastic
bottles that bob and spin seaward.

Thread

The surgeon's wife, stooping
in the border, caught
the tine of her fork, clogged
by muscled resistance; pulled
– out of the clump of Johnson's
Blue she was dividing –
leathery and flopping,
impaled, a toad.

A soft evening, the river
sliding past, silent.
Midges whined on their air-
cushion.

      The palpitating
sac of guts bulged,
swelled, the membranes tense
almost to spilling. Almost.

Cradling in laced hands
this alien hurt, lips
clamped tight, she imagined
whimpers, reptilian cries
the toad did not voice. Together,
surgeon's wife and surgeon
in the theatre of the kitchen
easing the guts back in
holding the quivering flap
with the back of a spoon
they stitched the mottled skin
with her finest needle
drawing a nylon thread.
Five sutures, and a knot.

Dark. The toad burrows

into the earth at the base
of a cardboard box. Sleeps,
perhaps: perhaps, throbbing,
waits, the encased fragile
organs replaced, but slightly
askew.

Day. The surgeon's wife
peers into the box.
She brings from the library
a book on toads, from the garden
worms, woodlice. The toad
touches nothing. Breathes.
She hovers, then moves
away. Another day passes.

Next evening, they tilt
the box, inch in a hand.
Pause. Rustle. Then the toad's
webbed pads imprint
the wrist, pressing hairs,
freckles, a shirt cuff
before mounting a tweed arm
to settle on a shoulder.
The wide mouth flicks
open, and closes. The eyes
gaze at his hosts, scanning
the huge faces, coarse pores,
sprouting hairs, unable
to recognize their smiles,
their triumphant tears.

Woman with a Pitcher of Milk

I am a flat surface, but you
don't see me like that. To you, I am
curves, solidity, a calm peasant face
absorbed in the work of my hands. But my hands
can't do anything. They do not hold
this jug (which is not a jug), they do not pour,
knead, pummel or shape the not-dough
you believe in. All I am is light.

The hands doing the work are what
you don't see. You don't see the eyes
that first saw me, an unfinished me,
a me-scrap you wouldn't recognize.
Saw, too, this light that makes curves
out of flat planes, that textures the cloth
over my breast, the skin of my forehead, the hair
escaping from my cap; light that tricks you
into believing in a table, a body, bread.

Who am I? Perhaps a patchwork
– scraps of women, glimpsed at windows, whisking
past in the street, strands of colour torn
from a hem, filched from the angle of a face?
Or one sample of the brisk mercantile city
I crossed this morning to the studio, threading
its ringing voices, its reek of ale and fish?
You scrutinize your catalogue, you stare
at the dance of photons swirling in this frame
as if to pierce the surface. But there is nothing
except the surface. Attend to that. Attend.

Recipe For a Folk Tale

The elements are simple. A woman; two
daughters, one a fast runner, the long
limbs flashing through the trees; the other, green
fingered as an April twig. A small house
in a clearing; vegetable patch; an apple tree
never known to fail.

The woman falls sick. Says nothing
to her daughters, conceals pain, fear;
goes one afternoon alone to the wise
woman at the far side of the wood – another
small house, red-brown roof, hedged
garden, well-planted.

She knocks. They talk. 'I cannot tell you' (says
the wisewoman) 'what to expect: some
with this sickness die soon; some linger
but die later; some recover. We cannot
tell why: some things must be left
for the great Mother of all.'

The fire rustles. 'What shall I do? I have
a garden to tend, daughters to advise.'
'Go home, plant your garden, advise your daughters
as you judge best. Do not despair; you may
live to harvest the crops you have planted.'
So they part; she leaves,

and through the thin sunlight of early spring
walks slowly under the tracery of trees
while her future travels towards her.
                              How will you
resolve it now? Shall she live, or die?
Shall the gardener pick an unremarkable
herb, steep it in water

to cure her mother? Shall the runner fetch (from a distant mountain) a gnarled root, some exotic spice, or perhaps simply a word of virtue? Decide: piece, pattern, brew as you like, following the known rules. Do not forget the apple tree.

The Box

She said

Don't open it
There is nothing
nothing for us there
Believe me, I have seen
the future full of blood
in the mirrors of the grass
the sky emptying
its arrows on us
heard muscle screaming
torn from bone
the cries of orphans,
and the suddenly childless

But he said

It is destiny, it is independence
the autonomy of a keen mind
the rational choice of fit survivors
of weapons in the race for supremacy
Someone has to win and by
God it's going to be –

Don't open the box, don't open

But he prised off the lid
with a stone chisel
and they watched a pottery
fragment twirl downwards
exploding into the whine of
howitzers, the blast of bombs
Suns of atoms shattering
flashed around them
Men fell in millions

children uncounted
the spermbanks emptied
ovaries melted

Looking into the bottom of the box
for what the gods had promised
she saw only despair.

After Babel

The day after work stopped on the building
when suddenly no one knew what to call
a hammer or a nail, when parrot screeches
and the growl of wolves clashed in the Tower
– after we'd all fallen silent again and no one
was even sobbing – the next morning, Grandmother
banged a ladle on a pan, called us together.
With wide gestures she invited us to sit
and then distributed slips of paper, tucking
them into our pockets, folding the flaps, frowning.

She laid her forefinger then on her lips
and pointed upward. Haltingly in the silence
our voices answered: Cielo. Ouranos.
Himmel. Sky. She nodded, flicked her hands
dispersing us to wander off alone.

We left the tower – what did it matter now?
– and set off on the paths across the fields
and woods. Rain fell. The sun shone.
Berries were ripe. A fox, rank and bushy,
crossed the path, wordless. Among the branches
swooped shadows and the purring flight of birds.
I named and named until my head was full
– then, hungry, astonished, eager, returned home
to share my hoard of words with all the others.

Grandmother had baked bread and cooked soup.
She fed us all, listening to our jargon
and the next day sent us out in groups.
It seemed she'd listened to our dreams as well
for Aleph, Beth and Gimel came with me
and Beth's child, who didn't have a name.
This time we travelled further. Each halt
along the way we gathered clumps of names

quarrelling occasionally, but quickly learning
to go for something everyone could say.

Sometimes we camped in the same place for weeks
and stocked our heads with movements: stretching, stooping,
leaving, returning, sleeping, walking, kissing.
I kept with Aleph, Gimel set up with Beth
so new and subtler movements were recorded:
the branches of a tree moved like a lover,
the earth was a mother. Likeness was born.

At times we met the others, traded words
and ate new foods. One day, at last, we thought
of the folded strips of paper. They were faded
now, and hard to read. We smoothed them out
and found a single word in our old language.
It was the same on every one (and try
as we might we never recalled another).
'Together', it said. 'Together'. 'Together'.

Nominal Aphasia

(Nominal aphasia is a condition in which the nouns – but not necessarily other types of words – cannot be accessed by the brain)

They are driving away from me
down the where they came from earlier
to visit me here in this
where I am

And cannot think of how to get away
or how I would manage
now that the
I had so easily once
have vanished from my
where they were always there ready
to roll off my long pink moist
where I keep it in my
where I eat and spit

Others such as wake shit sleep
have stayed but not the what
we all used in the old
the before
the before this happened

So perhaps they won't come again to see me
now I can't find the
whatever they were we always called them
to talk